NARROW
NET

SUMMER SPECIAL

THE DOUGLAS BAY HORSE TRAMWAY
by Stuart Mullan

Trammer *Mark* waits at the Derby Castle terminus with open toastrack tram 12.
Friends of Douglas Bay Horse Tramway

The Douglas Bay Horse Tramway is a truly unique survivor in the world of heritage transport. Having first opened in August 1876, it has operated continually along the seafront promenades of Douglas ever since (with the exception of a brief period of suspension during WW2). Whilst many towns and cities around the British Isles were replacing their horse-drawn trams with electric traction around the turn of the 20th century, the Douglas horse trams have continued to serve visitors to the capital of the Isle of Man and have long been a national icon.

History

The Douglas Bay Horse Tramway was the brainchild of 'retired' civil engineer Thomas Lightfoot. He was a native of Sheffield and retired to the Isle of Man in the early 1870s, briefly coming out of retirement in 1872 when he returned to Sheffield to build a horse tramway through the city. It's widely believed to be this which inspired him to consider building a tramway along the seafront of Douglas. Construction of the tramway appears to have been started before official approval was granted. Approval for the

1935-built tram No. 50 in service on 25 July 1971.
George Woods

opening was given on 7th August 1876 and the first services commenced the very same day with little celebration. The tramway opened as a single track with passing place, running from the Iron Pier (now known as Broadway) and Burn Mill Hill (now known as Summerhill). The original depot and stable facilities were built adjacent to the Lightfoot residence, Athol House. On opening day there were two double-deck tramcars, No.2 and 3, while No.1 was a single deck winter saloon delivered shortly after opening (not to be confused with the present-day No.1 which dates from 1913.

The tramway was a success from the off and the years that followed saw the tramway extended along Loch Promenade (January 1876) with further passing places added and further trams joining the fleet to keep up with demand. The current Summerhill Stables were opened in the winter of 1877 and the current depot at Strathallan in 1896. Eventually, the tramway became a double track along its full length. The tramway remained open during the First World War although the service was much reduced. A year-round service was in operation until November 1928 when the winter service was replaced by motor buses. Despite nearly all horse-drawn tramways being replaced by steam or electric traction by the 1930s, the Douglas line continued to prosper and in its 1930s heyday, the tramway carried 2,750,000 passengers in a single summer season and employed 135 horses and 50 tramcars. Trams would run every few minutes 'on demand'.

The Second World War saw the tramway close, as the tourists departed they were replaced by 'alien internees' as the seafront guest houses were transformed into an internment camp. The tramway horses were released for other uses and the tramcars were mothballed and placed into storage. At the cessation of hostilities, there was some debate as to whether or not the tramway would re-open. Thankfully Douglas Corporation made the decision to purchase 42 heavy horses from Ireland. Following their arrival, it was only a couple of months until services resumed in May 1946. Sadly, between 1948 and 1952 fourteen out-of-use tramcars were broken up, including many of the early double-deckers. By 1955 the only remaining double-decker no.14, no longer in use, left the island for the British Transport Museum (later part of the Science Museum) who restored it for static display.

The tramway continued to be a popular attraction for tourists visit the Island throughout the 1950s and 60s, but passenger numbers never quite recovered to their pre-war peak. A series of Royal visits in 1964 (The Queen Mother), 1965 (Princess Margaret), 1970 (Prince Philip) and 1972 (The Queen, Prince Philip, Princess Anne and Earl Mountbatten) publicised journeys made on the horse trams and appeared to spark some renewed interest in using the service, as passenger numbers again climbed past the 1,000,000 mark in 1974.

On 9 August 1976, the Douglas Bay Horse Tramway proudly celebrated its first 100 years of passenger services along Douglas promenades with special cavalcades of tramcars and horses. Double-decker No.14 returned to the Island to lead the main centenary procession, but was rightly considered a museum piece so was afterward mainly kept in the Derby Castle depot until in 1990 it was moved to the Manx Museum, Douglas, for more suitable permanent indoor display.

The tramway continued to be operated by Douglas Corporation (latterly known as Douglas Borough Council) throughout the 1980s and 90s. There was a resurgence of interest in the Island's railways and tramway during the 1990s, beginning with a Year of Railways event in 1993 that was staged to celebrate the 100th anniversary of the Manx Electric Railway.

Horses

The tramway horses, locally known as Trammers, are currently housed in Summer Hill Stables - originating from 1877 and thought to be one of the oldest working stables anywhere in the world that is still being used for their original purpose. The tramway employs around twenty horses with fifteen 'in service' and the remainder being younger horses in training. The training process can take anything up to five years, the horses stay with the tramway until they are around twenty years of age - each being assessed individually for retirement. Once they have completed their working life, most Trammers move to the Home of Rest for Old Horses located on Richmond Hill just outside of Douglas. The oldest and smallest trammer (and perhaps fastest) is Mark, the tallest is Steve, and the heaviest is Andrew. Two new horses have joined the tramway in 2017: Nelson is a three-year-old Shire and Blae is a young Clydesdale filly. In time, both of these horses will undergo training and join the working Trammers.

During the summer season, a normal working day for the horses consists of two return trips along the Promenades before retiring to the stables. This is in contrast to years gone by when, in the 1930s for example, it would not be unusual for horses to work seven or more return trips a day. During the closed season, the Trammers enjoy a winter break in fields on the hills above Onchan. Several of the Trammers will also compete in local ploughing matches which are held around the Island.

For more than twenty years, Bushy's Brewery has been a supporter of the tramway by supplying its spent malted barley from the brewing process to the stables as a protein supplement for the horses. Bushy's branding can be found on several tramcars and on the back of hi-visibility vests worn by staff. Okell's brewer Heron & Brearley have also supported the tramway, sponsoring the rebuild of 1883-built No.18 when it was restored to double deck form in 1988 after being used as a single deck saloon for many years.

Working roles for heavy draught horses not only helps to maintain health and fitness, it forms an important part of their breed conservation. Clydesdales remain on the Rare Breeds Survival Trust watchlist as a 'vulnerable' breed whilst Shires, although greater in number, are still considered an 'at risk' breed. There are only about 700 breeding Clydesdale mares left in the British Isles.

In years gone by the tramway ran a

The tallest horse on the tramway, *Steve*, is harnessed to car 43 at Derby Castle on 30th July 2016.

Oldest and smallest horse, *Mark*, on the return leg of his journey along the promenade with car 36 on 9th September 2015.

An 'action shot' of Rocky hauling tram 43 on 11th September 2015. Note the different advertising on the roof compared to that in the top photo on this page, taken a year later.

All: Friends of Douglas Bay Horse Tramway

breeding program for horses but as the service frequency has reduced, so too has the number of horses, to the point where it is now more cost effective to buy new horses. The most recent additions to the stables have all been bred in the north of the island.

Tramcars

A total of 51 tramcars have operated on the Douglas Bay Horse Tramway since its opening in 1876. We are fortunate in that some 25 of those cars, in both original form and converted types, have survived to the present day, although many in private ownership. The oldest surviving tramcar bought new for the Douglas Bay Horse Tramway is 'Toastrack' No. 11, built in 1886 by the Starbuck Car & Wagon Co of Birkenhead. It is currently stored in the north of the Island, albeit in poor condition.

Surviving double-deckers nos. 14 and 18 were both acquired second hand in 1887, but actually were built in 1883 and therefore are the oldest two tramcars. No.14 is on display in the Manx Museum and remains in near original form, whereas no.18 is still in service having been converted into a single deck saloon in 1903 and then back to a double-decker in 1988!

The youngest surviving tramcar, albeit in poor condition, is a more 'modern' all-weather convertible no.49, which was built in 1935 by Vulcan Motor & Engineering Co of Southport. All the other remaining tramcars are centenarians, built between 1888 and 1911, making them by far the largest and most historic collection of original horse-drawn tramcars in the world.

The Tramcar Depot at Strathallan was opened in 1896 as a single storey structure with storage space for up to 36 tramcars. The suite of offices on the first floor were added in 1935, but the inclusion of access stairwells reduced storage capacity to 27 tramcars. Following recent structural surveys, it has been determined that the Strathallan Tramcar Depot is life-expired and requires either significant repair or full replacement to continue in use. Therefore the Isle of Man Government has proposed the erection of a temporary (up to 5 years) alternative structure on nearly vacant development land to accommodate the remaining 13 tramcars and up to 20 horses.

Present Day

In January 2016, after 114 years of ownership and operation, Douglas Borough Council announced that it would no longer continue operating the Douglas Bay Horse Tramway due to financial constraints. The Council recorded a deficit of £268,000 for operating the service during 2015 and together with plans for the merging of the stables and depot into a new facility, the Council feared that the cost to ratepayers could reach £420,000 per year if the service was to continue. The news was met with widespread dismay among the many supporters of the tramway both on the island and further afield.

An online petition was launched, attracting several thousand signatures in support of keeping the service. In the first few days of the campaign a number of local politicians came out in support of the horse tramway and a committee was formed to look at all of the available options. This included the former owners Douglas Borough Council, Manx National Heritage and Isle of Man Railways (the operators of the Island's three other nationalised heritage railways).

Happily, a way forward was found, initially for the 2016 season only, to retain the horse tramway. Isle of Man Railways (a division of the Isle of Man Government Department of Infrastructure) took over the operation on a season-long loan from Douglas Borough Council with 13 tramcars and 22 horses available for service. The season got underway several weeks earlier than in previous years on 30th April and services ran until 30th October, around a month later than in recent years. Perhaps the biggest change under the new operator was that services no longer ran seven days a week during the shoulder season. The end of season results showed that the longer season and selected

Covered toastrack No. 36 approaches the Sea Terminal on 1st July 2016 in the care of *Una*.

The oldest tram is double-decker No. 18, built in 1883 and acquired second hand in 1887. It is seen here behind *William*.

Enclosed Saloon No. 27 heads for the Sea Terminal with *Philip* in charge.

All: Friends of Douglas Bay Horse Tramway

Our final view of the Sea Terminal end of the line sees *William* and Tram 43 nearing the terminus on 19th July 2016.
Friends of Douglas Bay Horse Tramway

days of operation had paid off. The operating subsidy had been slashed to approximately £60,000 thanks to a large rise in passenger revenue. Passenger numbers were also up with a total of 69,542 passenger journey completed.

In July 2016 Tynwald (the parliament of the Isle of Man) agreed to support the Douglas Bay Horse Tramway for a further two seasons (2017 & 2018) as a trial to see if the case could be made for retaining the tramway in the longer term. In recent years Douglas Promenade, along which the tramway runs, has been the subject of much political debate and at times heated controversy in relation to proposals for the rebuilding of the seafront. The roadway suffers from subsidence in places due to being built on reclaimed land and the concrete 'pads' upon which the promenade is built are reported to have shifted and cracked. In April 2016 plans were submitted that would have seen the tramway shortened in length and the half mile section along Loch Promenade closed. Thankfully as well as supporting two further seasons of operation, Tynwald also supported an amendment to retain the tramway along the full length of the Promenade.

In August 2016 six surplus tramcars were offered for sale by auction as Douglas Borough Council looked to divest itself of the operation. Thirteen tramcars were chosen for service by Isle of Man Railways (nine 'service' trams and four in a 'Museum Fleet' for use on special occasions)

Although the future of the Douglas Bay Horse Tramway has been uncertain during the past couple of years, it seems that it may now have a fighting chance of survival, as an important part of the Manx heritage transport network supporting the Island's visitor economy.

The Friends

Despite its uniqueness in heritage transport terms, until recently the tramway did not have a dedicated support group. The Friends of Douglas Bay Horse Tramway was formed in 2014 as an independent volunteer community group (independent of government and any other organisation) with the principal aim to help promote and support the continued operation of the tramway.

Among other activities, we maintain an online information website at www.friendsofdbht.org, provide volunteer guides for tours of Summer Hill Stables and publish a regular e-journal with all the latest news from the tramway and stables. We also hold regular meetings with the Isle of Man Government and other stakeholders in the tramway. It's easy and free to become a Friend of DBHT, visit our website for details.

We finish with two views of the Derby Castle terminus. (*Above*) Tram 43 with the tram depot behind, and (*below*) *Una* and tram 44 set off on another journey to the Sea Terminal, with the Manx Electric Railway infrastructure visible on the right.

Both: Friends of Douglas Bay Horse Tramway

TEIFI VALLEY PHOENIX
by Iain McCall

The revived railway - ALAN GEORGE and both serviceable coaches wait for customers at Henllan on 18th March 2017.
All photographs by the Author

Introduction

In recent times, the Teifi Valley Railway has had the most chequered existence of any heritage railway in the UK. From the completion of its extension in 2009, things entered a downward spiral culminating in the rails being ripped up in 2014. Now the rebuilding process is well underway...

History

The history of the railway begins in the era of Brunel's 7ft $0\frac{1}{4}$in broad gauge, being conceived in the 1850s as part of the Carmarthen & Cardigan Railway - a line which, like many in the Victorian era, was destined never to link the places in its title.

However the broad gauge era came to an end with the conversion of the C&C to standard gauge in 1872, by which date the line had reached Llandysul, some miles short of the current Teifi Valley Railway trackbed.

It was not until July 1895, under Great Western Railway auspices, that the branch opened along what is now the TVR trackbed and reached Newcastle Emlyn, destined to be the terminus of the line.

The line then settled in to its role as a far-flung outpost of the GWR's empire, but the nationalisation of the railways in 1948 brought with it impending doom, and the branch lost its passenger services in 1952, the last train being on 13th September that

The classic preservation era view - SGT MURPHY takes water at the original preservation era station site at Henllan. This was just to the west of the later (and current) terminus.

year.

Freight services continued however, with intermediate stations (including the TVR's base at Henllan) being closed to goods traffic in 1965, and the branch as a whole being closed upon the cessation of goods traffic to Newcastle Emlyn on 28th September 1973.

Preservation

By the time of the closure in 1973, there was a preservation group, the Teifi Valley Railway Preservation Society, which was actively seeking the preservation of the whole line from Carmarthen to Newcastle Emlyn.

This Society eventually split into two, one group, the Gwili Railway Preservation Society, preserving a section of the standard gauge just north of Carmarthen. The second, the Dyfed Railway Company, was inspired by the success of the Bala Lake Railway at operating a 2ft gauge line along an ex-standard gauge trackbed, and decided to follow suit, basing its operations at Henllan on the Newcastle Emlyn branch, with the stated intention of reopening the seven mile section between Llandysul and Newcastle Emlyn. This latter became what is now known as the Teifi Valley Railway.

Work on the 2ft gauge line started in 1981, and by 1983 had progressed sufficiently for the line to be reopened to Pontprenshitw, further extensions following to Llandyfriog (1987), Pont Goch (2006) and Henllan GWR station (2009).

Pont Goch is the limit of westward extension in the short term, as the bridge over the River Teifi at this point ('Pont' being Welsh for 'bridge') requires complete rebuilding before trains can cross. Nevertheless, the railway retains aspirations to reach Newcastle Emlyn.

The major obstacle yet to be tackled - the collapsed bridge immediately west of Pont Goch halt will need to be rebuilt before the railway can reach its ultimate goal of Newcastle Emlyn.

The collapse

The crisis began in 2013, with a shortage of volunteers and management personnel in a number of areas, which ultimately led to the operation of the railway being leased to a third party with no previous experience of operating railways. During the year, various maintenance requirements were not attended to.

Then in April 2014, the TVR was subject to a visit from the Railway Inspector, which noted significant defects with the railway's administration. After a second visit in June, the railway agreed to a voluntary closure to allow the defects to be rectified.

However, a more significant problem was the nature of the lease, as the leaseholder was not permitted to operate the railway under the terms of the Light Railway Order.

The leaseholder's response to this was unexpected - he dismantled the first half mile of track, and commenced the operation of a 'road train' along the dismantled trackbed. The remainder of the track, whilst not being dismantled, was severely damaged by equipment used to harvest logs from forestry adjacent to the line.

Rebirth and rebuilding

In November 2014, a new group, which included a number of 'old TVR faces' took over the management and operation of the line.

From this date, rebuilding of the railway, both physically and organisationally, has continued. The line reopened as far as Forest Halt in August 2016, and is in progress beyond there to the next goal of Pontprenshitw, which is intended to become more of a "destination" whilst work continues to rebuild to Pont Goch.

Two views which are still to be recreated... Above is ALAN GEORGE running round its train at the line's western terminus of Pont Goch, and below SGT MURPHY waits departure time from Henllan. This loco is currently being overhauled.

ALAN GEORGE waits for the photographer at Forest Halt. Behind the train can be seen the wagons of the permanent way train, and beyond them is the 'head of steel', pictured below with the trackbed towards Pontprenshitw disappearing around the corner.

The way ahead - ALAN GEORGE prepares to return to Henllan from Forest Halt on 18th March 2017.

FFESTINIOG RAILWAY THEN AND NOW

Double Fairlie JAMES SPOONER is soon to be recreated by the FR. The original is pictured above on The Cob, whilst below are the drawings for the new boiler currently under construction.

Both: FR

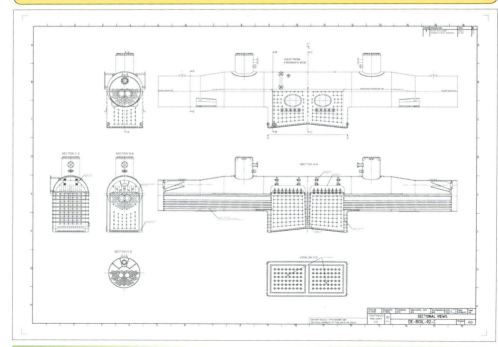

Hunslet LINDA is pictured above during its pre-preservation career on the Penrhyn Railway in the 1950s, and below in 2011 at Minffordd Yard - the latter view made possible by the fitting of an auxiliary oil tank under the cab to replace the preservation-era tender.
FR / Andrew Thomas

Gravity trains on the FR then and now - note the increase in the number of brakemen!
FR / Peter Donovan

Two views of Porthmadog, the first from an engraving c1840.

FR / Andrew Thomas

OVERSEAS INTERLUDE 1: MYANMAR
by Bryan Acford

Above: YC629 departs Pyuntaza with a train for Bago on 9th January during the rail-tour organised by Farrail.

Below: ST784 at the site of the former Mokpalin depot. The turntable has recently been re-instated here so would be useful for any steam specials.

All photographs by the Author

Above: YD964 arrives at Theinzeik just after sunrise on 16th January with a chartered freight from Mottama – Bago.

Below: YD964 crosses a river bridge south of Mayangone on 12th January with a chartered freight train from Bago – Mottama.

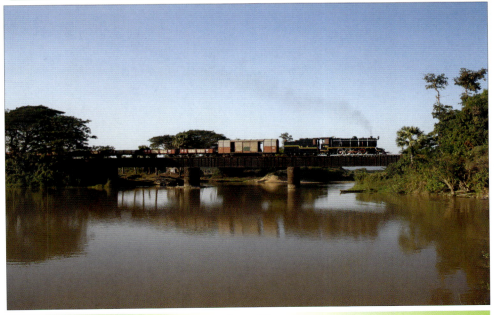

Above: ALSTOM Bo-Bo-Bo DF1228 with Train 86 the Moulmein – Bago mixed waits at Hinin Pale to cross a Moulmain bound express on 16th January. Note that the first 3 vehicles are locally converted goods wagons with wooden bench seats fitted.

Below: DF2071 from the latest batch of Dalian (China) built 2000hp Bo-Bo-Bo Diesel Electrics, and carrying a revised livery, hauling a rake of Chinese built carriages departs Bago Train 5 the 1500 Yangon – Mandalay overnight train on 8th January.

Above: Former Indian Railways DF1336 arrives at Zingyaik with Train 89 from Yangon – Moulmein on 15th January.

Below: Re-engined ALSTHOM Bo-Bo-Bo DF1200.05 arrives at Nuangpattaya with a loaded stone train from Zingyaik, on 10th January. 10 years previously this would have been in the hands of a YD class 2-8-2.

RENAISSANCE AT KEMPTON PARK
by Tony Eaton

Newly arrived DARENT takes its first load of passengers around the Hanworth Loop, 31st August 2013. The horse is unperturbed probably realising that in future he can look forward to extra carrots from the passengers.

All photos from MWBRS Archives

In the beginning

Regular travellers on the M3 to or from London will be familiar with the two tall chimneys just south of the elevated section of the A316 road about a mile on the London side of Sunbury. These formerly served the coal fired boilers of the Kempton Park Steam Pumping engines which have been preserved and are operated on some weekends. However the steam is now produced by a gas fired boiler and the chimneys themselves will never be seen clagging. On the northern side of the road and less obvious to the passer-by, there is now a circle of narrow gauge railway track on which coal-fired steam hauled trains can be seen running. This is the Hanworth Loop of the embryonic Hampton & Kempton Waterworks Railway which operates every weekend from early spring until late autumn. To understand how this has come about one has to go back to the mid 19th century to see how London's water supply developed. As the city grew its need for clean water increased rapidly and the flatlands of West Middlesex proved ideal for the construction of reservoirs to store and purify water extracted from the relatively unpolluted River Thames above the tidal boundary at Teddington. A number of private companies were involved in this but all were merged into the publicly owned Metropolitan Water Board (MWB) at the beginning of the 20th Century. Nowadays of course it is known as Thames Water and is once again in private hands.

All this water needed distribution and a number of steam-powered pumping stations were built. These included one by the Thames at Hampton, and another at Kempton Park which was used to pump water across to North London. Coal was necessary to power the boilers and waterborne supplies were preferred as the cost was less than for coal delivered by rail. Thameside Hampton was supplied by barge but Kempton Park was initially served by a private siding from the then London & South Western Railway branch to Shepperton.

Decline, closure and Rebirth

Over the years there were supply problems both with water and rail, and in 1912 the Metropolitan Water Board decided to build a narrow gauge railway to transport coal from the Thames at Hampton to Kempton Park. This would also allow Hampton to be supplied by rail via the Shepperton branch if necessary, thus providing backup supplies to both locations. The 2' gauge line was about 2 miles long and to operate it Kerr Stuart supplied three 0-4-2T locos - HAMPTON, KEMPTON and SUNBURY. It was completed in late 1916 and quietly went about its business until sometime in the 1940s. No record exists of the actual closure date but it is thought that its use slowly declined with the gradual replacement of the older reciprocating pumping engines

SUNBURY poses at Kempton Park probably in the early years of the railway.

by turbines. The locos were scrapped as was most of the infrastructure. However much of the route can still be traced and the occasional length of rail is still visible. The standard gauge connection to the Shepperton line was abandoned in the 1960s.

The Kempton Park site was the subject of a major development in the 1920s when the MWB constructed an engine house with two of the largest triple-expansion pumping engines ever built. Brought into use in 1928 this provided steam-pumped drinking water to the residents of North London until it was replaced in the early 1980s. Luckily the engine house was preserved and is now in the care of the Kempton Great Engines Trust (KGET), a registered charity, on a long lease from Thames Water. It is open to the public and one of the engines has been restored and is steamed on several weekends each year.

In the 1980s there had also been a number of proposals to reinstate a railway on the old trackbed which is almost entirely on Thames Water property, but none had progressed beyond the planning stage. Thames Water were always supportive in facilitating any scheme but were unable to become directly involved. However, encouraged by their success with the Great Engines project and looking for a new challenge, a group of members formed the Metropolitan Water Board Railway Society (MWBRS) in 2003 with the objective of restoring as much as possible of the original narrow gauge railway from Kempton Park towards Hampton. There were (and still are!) many obstacles to overcome - the route comes under the jurisdiction of three local councils and almost all of it is on private Thames Water land. This latter means that strict environmental rules apply, but it also means that en route to Hampton it follows a surprisingly rural path passing a wildlife conservation area which is otherwise inaccessible to the public. Developments at the Hampton end of the line mean that the restored railway is unlikely to quite reach its original destination of the coal wharf at Hampton which is itself now defunct. However it should be possible to run for about 1½ miles to a point adjacent to the Lower Sunbury Road and almost within sight of its original destination.

Work starts

The MWBRS soon attracted enough members and volunteers to establish that the project stood a good chance of success and a base was quickly established adjacent to the Great Engine House at Kempton Park. Partly situated under the elevated A316 road, it provides ample working and storage space and is protected from the worst of the weather.

It was realised that building a railway through Thames Water land would involve a number of administrative hurdles. Obviously a lease would be needed from Thames Water, there are environmental factors and the line would also run through three local government districts – Hounslow, Richmond and Spelthorne. All parties involved proved supportive but it was quickly realised that it would not be possible to immediately start laying track towards Hampton.

Luckily members of the KGET, many of whom also belong to the MWBRS, have always been enthusiastic supporters. They view the presence of an operating railway as an attractive addition to the Kempton Park site and likely to increase their own visitor numbers. Part of the land leased to them is a meadow immediately to the north of the elevated road which was not being used except for grazing horses. They suggested that this could be the site for the first phase of the railway in advance of the MWBRS getting its own lease. This offer was quickly accepted as the MWBRS were determined to make a start. At about the same time the opportunity arose to acquire track and pointwork from the unlikely location of a modern business park near Cambridge. Also included was a bridge - an essential requirement as the railway needs to cross a water course at the very start of its route towards Hampton. This acquisition was funded with the help of a generous interest

Early days of construction. Petrol hydraulic HOUNSLOW on a short works train, 17th June 2011.

Bridge and trackwork await removal and collection at the Welding Institute near Cambridge, 5th October 2009. An improbable sight at a late 20th Century business park where it had originally been constructed as a training project. An impressive structure which the Kempton volunteers succeeded in dismantling and transporting back to Kempton Park ready for reuse – no mean feat.

free loan from one of the members. It was time to get going!

For obvious reasons a circular layout was selected and configured in such a way as to facilitate the future breakout towards Hampton. The horses would remain relatively undisturbed safely fenced off from the encircling trackwork. Track laying proceeded during 2011/12 and some rolling stock was acquired. This included two coaches from Exbury in Devon which were restored and fitted with completely new bodies. As construction neared completion in late 2012 thoughts turned towards motive power since at that time the only locomotive available was HOUNSLOW a very small petrol driven locomotive built and on loan from Science Projects, an educational charity. This was perfect for moving wagons of ballast around but not powerful enough to haul trainloads of passengers. Luckily, the London Museum of Water & Steam at

THOMAS WICKSTEED on a crew training run, 21st April 2013. In the background the station building, at this stage a tent, is being prepared for the official opening a few weeks later. The station building was later upgraded to a garden shed donated by the local garden centre and more recently to a permanent building.

Hampton & Kempton Waterworks Railway
Proposed route to Hydes Field, Hampton

In the short period before the Kew stock departed a double header was arranged. Here both locos haul the Kew coach and the newly restored Devon coach – at that time the combined passenger stock of both railways.

Kew Bridge who have a short demonstration line, were at that time unable to use their railway because of rebuilding work funded by a Lottery grant. They generously offered to loan their rolling stock for the summer of 2013. This included ALISTER a small diesel and a steam loco THOMAS WICKSTEED built as recently as 2008 – the same year as TORNADO but not quite as famous! Help from Kew also proved invaluable in training the volunteers at Kempton Park ready for railway operation.

Opening and Consolidation

Thus it was possible to open the Hanworth Loop to the public in May 2013 with steam. For legal reasons a separate limited company, the Hampton & Kempton Waterworks Railway, was set up to run the railway, but the MWBRS provides all the volunteers to operate and maintain it.

After a successful first season which proved the attraction of steam, the two visiting locos were returned to Kew, but not before a member had bought their own steam loco and generously placed it on loan for the duration of its boiler ticket which expires in 2019. DARENT was built in 1903 for Provan gasworks in Glasgow to 2'6" gauge with a cutdown cab. Not very elegant, but after entering private ownership it was rebuilt and regauged to 2' in 2003 and is now a rather good looking centenarian which has proved very reliable in service.

In retrospect, building the Hanworth Loop acted as an essential training project for volunteers many of whom had no previous experience of railway construction and established the credibility of the railway as a professional organisation. Since then there has been a period of consolidation. Further rolling stock and two small diesels (mainly for works traffic) have been acquired and services have been expanded particularly through holding special events such as Santa and Halloween specials. As a result passenger numbers have increased steadily and in 2016 over 6000 passengers were carried.

So what of the future?

So far a short working railway has been constructed almost entirely through the efforts and generosity of members and volunteers. A number of relatively modest grants have been received from local organisations which have helped with specific projects such as carriage restoration. In excess of £40,000 has been contributed either through grants or donations not to mention the loan of valuable assets such as DARENT. Operationally the railway covers its day-to-day running costs but it will never generate enough surplus to allow extension of the line to the ultimate goal of Hampton, the total cost of which has been estimated to be about £1,500,000. However in 2016 an application to become a registered charity was granted which opens up the potential to apply for grants from many more organisations such as the lottery. Given the relatively modest start that has been made it is unrealistic to expect to raise this amount of finance immediately so the project has been broken down into a number of phases. These see the building of the line to Hampton, a branch to Kempton Park mainline station and the development of a visitor and information centre. Negotiations with Thames Water are in their final stages before construction of the first phase can be started in earnest. However some preliminary ground clearance has been done and the junction from the Hanworth Loop has been installed. For obvious reasons this is called the 'Breakout Project'. It will see the line crossing under the elevated A316 and heading towards Hampton. Initially on a new alignment it will rejoin the original trackbed before reaching Bunny Lane where a halt is planned.

How you can help

Apart from the obvious need for finance plans rely heavily on using volunteer labour – more than 20,000 hours are needed to complete the line to Hampton. At the same time trains will be running over a gradually extending route so the need for volunteers

The way ahead. Preliminary clearance work in the densely wooded section towards Hampton, 27th April 2016. It is hard to believe this is west Middlesex.

will increase as the railway develops – it is intended that the railway will continue to be run entirely by volunteers. At the moment there are about forty regulars many of whom have been involved from the beginning and some attend on all three working days each week – Sundays, Tuesdays and Thursdays. This long term enthusiasm is very gratifying but more volunteers are needed.

A wide range of skills is required. These range from the obvious ones required for railway construction and operation but there are many other ways in which to contribute. Good catering is important for any visitor attraction, but assistance is also needed for many of the 'back office' functions that are essential for success. These include planning, finance, book keeping, general administration and IT. Clearly construction work and operational type activities have to be done on site, but most of the other work can be done remotely so living close by may not be important.

If you think you could help even occasionally the first step is to contact mwbrsoffice@gmail.com or see the website www.hamptonkemptonrailway.org.uk

Prospective volunteers are welcome to come and look round on any of the working days, but because the railway is on a secure Thames Water site, this needs to be arranged beforehand to avoid any delay on arrival.

Two views of the start of the breakout towards Hampton. Hunslet-Jenbach No. 53 delivers ballast for the newly installed junction with the Hanworth Loop, 21st February 2017. The diesel was one of two acquired from Hong Kong where they had been used for a tunnelling project. The shipping container on the left is the railway's steam shed.

NARROW GAUGE 2016

We begin our photographic survey of 2016 with two Lynton & Barnstaple replicas. Above is $12\frac{1}{4}$" gauge YEO at Barmouth Ferry on the Fairbourne Railway, and below is 'big brother' LYD outside Boston Lodge on the Ffestiniog Railway.

Both: Peter Donovan

ROGER (Kerr, Stuart 3128/1918) poses on the Garden Railway at Statfold Barn on 10th September, whilst (*below*) fellow Kerr, Stuart product JOAN is coaled at Llanfair Caereinion on 23rd August.

Both: Peter Donovan

A locomotive which rarely features in the railway press is Corris Railway No. 5 ALAN MEADEN, seen here at Maespoeth with a demonstration freight train during the 29th May Gala Day.

Peter Donovan

Another Gala Day demonstration goods was that hauled by Penrhyn-liveried 'Quarry Hunslet' WINIFRED, seen with matching slate wagons during the Bala Lake Railway's event on 26th August.

Peter Donovan

Our journey now takes us across the sea to the Isle of Man for the Groudle Glen Railway Gala on 31st July 2016 where we see (*above*) the 'Steamplex' at Lhen Coan, and (*below*) the line's original locos SEA LION and POLAR BEAR together at Sea Lion Rocks.
Both: Andrew Budd

Finally in this selection, the Alan Keef Open Day on 17th September saw PETER PAN and WOTO in action on the Lea Line (*above*) and (*below*) MR 2014 DALMUNZIE.
Both: Andrew Budd

FAIRBOURNE 15 INCH RESURGENCE
by Graham Billington

KATIE waits with the 15 inch gauge train whilst COUNT LOUIS stands on the adjacent line during the May 2016 "Centenary of Steam" event.

All photos by the Author

Back in the early nineteen eighties, the Fairbourne Railway entered a turbulent period. With a new owner, the character of the line was about to change, not it must be said, for the first time, since it is in the nature of miniature railways to be more susceptible to change than their bigger brothers. History tells us that the Fairbourne had already led an existence of a somewhat cyclical nature, with periods of new impetus and capital interspersed with troughs of under investment. Changes of gauge were not unknown either in the line's story. Starting as an industrial horse tramway of two feet gauge back in 1896, the original purpose of the railway had been to convey building materials from a brickyard adjacent to the Cambrian Railway to a new speculative holiday village. This was the brainchild of a Scotsman, Arthur McDougall, whose idea was to establish a seaside haven for people who lived and worked in the bustle of the Midlands. Having made his name in the flour industry, Arthur was taking advantage of the birth of tourism, made possible by the development of main line railway travel, alongside others like Savin and Andrews. With the village completed and given an

The line's first steam locomotive, PRINCE EDWARD OF WALES, now renamed KING GEORGE, on static display on the traverser at Fairbourne on its return visit.

English name, a Fair Bourne on Cardigan Bay, the line was converted to a passenger carrying link to the Barmouth Ferry, retaining the track gauge and horse motive power.

By the advent of the First World War, the railway had sunk into the first of the troughs and was rescued by Bassett-Lowke as part of another innovative thrust to make miniature railways part of the tourism experience. The line was re-gauged to 15 inches and steam power came to Fairbourne. World War Two, was the next watershed with the line almost obliterated and in need of resuscitation by another benefactor, John Wilkins of Servis washing machine fame. Over the next thirty odd years he built up the railway as one of the premier 15 inch gauge lines in Britain until in the early eighties, investment was once more necessary for the survival of the line.

Enter John Ellerton, pop star, entrepreneur and the man with the money to revive the Fairbourne's fortunes. There is no doubt that he saved the railway, but it was the way in which it was done that caused controversy.

The line was re-gauged to 12 ¼ inches, and the rolling stock, including the much loved locomotives was sold off and dispersed. They were replaced with four new steam locos and thirty new carriages, changing the character of the line. The volunteers were also replaced initially with paid staff and they, too, dispersed. Many of them did not care for the new look of the railway and went elsewhere. Eventually, the Fairbourne was to find its present set-up with ownership transferred to a charitable trust and a small nucleus of paid staff supported by the Fairbourne Railway Preservation Society. But the problem remained. The new devotees of the 12 ¼ inch gauge line included some who had previously loved the 15 inch gauge incarnation, but many others still shunned the new Fairbourne and longed

Two of the "Centenary of Steam" visitors - COUNT LOUIS (*above*) and KATIE.

for a return to the old days. In recent times, under the stewardship of Manager Murray Dods, plans were set in motion to bring the two together.

Celebrating the heritage was the key. The problem was the difference in gauges. We could bring in former Fairbourne favourites, but would not be able to run them unless....

It would require significant investment, but dual gauge track would enable the railway to bring back 15 inch gauge engines for gala days. There was one obvious place to start it. The siding nearest Beach Road was on the trackbed of the original terminus line from 1916. A small beginning was made, with a short length of dual gauge track laid. It was not easy. The sleepers had to be replaced with longer ones and extra rail bought in. It was, however, proved a success when successive gala days saw the return of KATIE, GWRIL and WHIPPIT QUICK along with first time visitors, SOONY and Rhyl's Cagney No. 44. These events brought in crowds of visitors and emboldened the railway to build on these foundations. The dual gauge track was extended up Beach Road as far as the first crossing by the Springfield Hotel. It was also discovered that when John Ellerton first took over the line, intending to regauge, he initially ran it as 15 inch gauge for an interim period. As a result, the track in the workshop and on the traverser was already dual gauge. Once the workshop track was dug out from the covering of concrete, a purpose built dual gauge point and a crossing were put in to link this with the dual gauge siding with a further dual gauge section from the sector plate to the station throat, while a new island platform was built for the 15 inch gauge trains.

The infrastructure was in place by the end of the winter of 2015/16. GWRIL and two former Fairbourne coaches arrived on loan from Windmill Farm towards the end of 2015. They would be used for testing the new track formation and would form the train for the 2016 gala to mark 100 years of steam at Fairbourne. One of the iconic steam locos had already been a proven success on the new dual gauge track, so was a popular choice for a second visit. The 2-4-2 built by Trevor Guest to Ernest Twining's design in 1954 had at first run at Dudley Zoo, before being transferred into the private collection of Captain Hewitt in Anglesey and eventually acquired by the Fairbourne in 1965 where it ran until 1984. KATIE was to return but herein lay the first problem. KATIE had by now been sold by Austin Moss, with whom the railway had agreed the return of the much loved Guest built loco. New owners, the Kirklees Light Railway, were happy to honour the arrangement and for KATIE to return for the second time.

The next obvious choice was the loco that had been the mainstay of the line from its purchase in 1925 from the estate of the late Count Louis Zborowski until its eventual removal from the line in 1987. COUNT LOUIS, a Bassett-Lowke Class 30 Little Giant 4-4-2 was now a touring engine with no fixed home, but Michael Whitehouse agreed for its return for the Fairbourne Centenary of Steam Gala.

The final choice was to be the return after an absence of over 90 years of the original engine from 1916. PRINCE EDWARD OF WALES was a Bassett-Lowke Class 20 Little Giant Atlantic built for the opening of the line. The loco, now renamed KING GEORGE had not made a public appearance for some time but was undergoing restoration. Time was now the enemy and sadly time ran out before Little Giant number 22 could be made ready to run, but the iconic loco was delivered to Fairbourne for static display. So close a call was it, that Austin Moss built and fitted the running boards in the Fairbourne workshops on the Friday night for the Saturday morning opening of the gala!

For the first time, a gala Guide was prepared and arrangements made for a Gala DVD to be made for sale after the event. The first day was also to mark the launch of the first new book on the history of the line for twenty years. This, too, proved to be a race against time. The manuscript for The Fairbourne Railway, A Centenary of Steam, had been lost with the theft of a computer and the author was about to depart for Japan. Backup copies were swiftly put together and the completed books picked up from the printer on the night before the gala. At Barmouth Ferry, a bigger marquee had been ordered and the new dual gauge 5 inch and 7¼ inch gauge miniature railway was ready to be inaugurated.

On the first day, the sun shone and the temperature rose just as it did in everyone's memories of childhood seaside holidays at Fairbourne. The crowds were the size of crowds seen on the old films of the lines in the golden days of the fifties. The resident "new" locos (fast approaching their 40th birthdays), YEO, RUSSELL and SHERPA, together with diesels TONY and GWRIL hauled eight and nine coach trains on the main line. On the 15 inch gauge, two ex-Fairbourne coaches, 16 and 20, were hauled by COUNT LOUIS and KATIE. On the traverser KING GEORGE celebrated his own 100th birthday with a bottle of champagne. Henry Greenly did the honours in the shape of Austin Moss. At Barmouth Ferry, the miniature railway proved a success with live steam, with a fairground organ for added nostalgia. John Campbell's excavator line, Mick Mobley's Hornby 3 rail railway and Gwernol Fach, the 16 mm layout attracted crowds to the marquee, while outside on display stood a restored 1961 Berkeley classic car.

The crowds that came broke records for the 12¼ inch gauge railway. The enthusiasts and former volunteers came and enjoyed themselves, liking what they saw. Essentially they found that the railway had not changed that much. The journey was the same and the line run by people who loved the Fairbourne. The old and the new had successfully reunited, the resurgent railway was once again being featured in the railway press and everyone was so pleased that we did it all again a couple of months later in Yorkshire, when the Kirklees Light Railway held a Fairbourne in the Hills event. Renaming their railway and stations and reuniting five former Fairbourne locos, SIAN, KATIE, COUNT LOUIS, GWRIL, WHIPPIT QUICK and one new one, SHERPA. But that's another story.

Fairbourne in the Hills - COUNT LOUIS, SIAN and KATIE at Kirklees.

"Centenary of Steam" highlights - a 15 inch triple-header, led by an out of steam KING GEORGE, with COUNT LOUIS and KATIE behind. Later in the day, KING GEORGE poses for photographs on the 15 inch gauge running line.

OVERSEAS INTERLUDE 2: MIDWINTER HARZ
by Michael Reilly

With China's Sandaoling apparently set to see a significant reduction in steam working, if not its complete end, by mid-May, Germany's Harz narrow gauge system may soon justifiably claim to offer the most intensive regular steam-working anywhere in the world.

With a timetable that calls for 6 locos in steam even on midweek days in winter, quite apart from special workings, there is almost always plenty of interest for the enthusiast, especially at the junction station of Drei Annen Hohne, where the line to the summit of the Brocken diverges from that across the Harz to Nordhausen, as these photographs, taken over the weekend from 24 – 26 February show.

On 24 February an overnight fall of snow remained undisturbed by wheels on rails or even animal tracks and the normal path of the morning railcar from Wernigerode to Eisfelder Talmuhle had been commandeered by the snowplough, seen here waiting the road up the Brocken out of Drei Annen Hohne station.

All photographs by the Author

It was till snowing heavily 90 minutes later as 2-10-2T 99-7243-1 storms the bank out of Drei Annen Hohne with the first passenger train of the day bound for the Brocken.

By mid-morning the snow had stopped falling, the sun had come out and briefly caught 99-7235-7 as it pulled away from Schierke station with the second train of the day.

Drei Annen Hohne station is over 300 metres higher above sea level than Wernigerode and there was not the slightest hint of any snow, on the ground or in the air, as 99-7234-0 rounds the horseshoe curve at Steinern Renne at the start of an unbroken climb of 9km to Drei Annen Hohne. The following day this loco would disgrace itself. The sun had brought weekend crowds to visit the Brocken but the loco failed near the summit with a heavily loaded train, trapping two trains above it and bringing operations to the Brocken to a summary halt for almost the rest of the day.

By 26 February a steady thaw had removed most traces of snow from Drei Annen Hohne and 99-7239-9 is bathed in sunshine as it gets the mid-day departure for Brocken underway, with drain cocks wide open.

Locos on the Harz system normally operate smokebox first southbound, so a view such as this is unusual. On the day 99-7245-6 was the loco working the two daily steam turns over the section between Drei Annen Hohne and Eisfelder Talmuhle, from where it had recently arrived and is taking water before returning with the 12.40 departure. On the right, 99-7232-4 has just arrived with a train from Wernigerode and will shortly continue to the Brocken with the 12.45 train, formed of the carriages 99-7245-6 had previously brought from Nordhausen.

The snow might have all but vanished from Drei Annen Hohne by the afternoon of 26 February, but the Brocken is the highest point in northern Germany and the station there is almost 600 metres higher above sea level than Drei Annen Hohne and conditions remained decidedly wintry. 99-7232-4 pauses while running round its train. Three more trains will follow it down before the end of the day.

TEESDALE 15 INCH GAUGE VISITORS
by the Friends of the Thorpe LR

FLYING SCOTSMAN, having bypassed the station, is curving round the near loop on a busy day at Whorlton. Note the well-maintained track.

the late Dave Holroyde

Four miles east of Barnard Castle in Teesdale there has existed a 15" gauge railway since 1971. Between then and its closure in 2005 as a commercial operation it had resident locomotives but just one visiting engine, albeit a scale model of a famous one. After reopening on a limited basis in 2013 with the landowner's agreement it has had one then, more recently, two resident locomotives but already hosted three visiting engines. More are likely in the future.

When the railway opened as the Whorlton Lido Railway it had a Bassett Lowke 4-4-2 KING GEORGE joined in 1972 by diesel WENDY. Five years later regional TV and newspapers reported a new steam locomotive was to undergo trials at Whorlton. The reason for such coverage? It was a highly-detailed 1/4 size scale model of FLYING SCOTSMAN, already well known but by then a celebrity after over a decade of preservation running. Bill Stewart had

An impressive 15" gauge FLYING SCOTSMAN waits at Whorlton station for its next departure.

the late Dave Holroyde

built it at his Washington Sheet Metal Works factory some 30 miles away. Bill supervised its unloading at Whorlton on June 9th. Media coverage attracted even more people, like the author, to this popular day trippers' spot. It made an impressive sight in its apple green LNER livery. It was quite a size too with the locomotive 12 ft long and the tender 7 ft 6 in. Like the original it had three cylinders. Weight was estimated at 4 tons.

The author recalls a competent ride round the dog bone shaped circuit. After a short period of trials it returned to its builder. That September it ran at the Ravenglass centenary celebrations. It returned to Whorlton on June 12th 1977 where it stayed for a longer visit until 1979. It was used infrequently, usually being driven by site/railway owner Raymond Dunn or Bill Stewart. One day another gentleman who had his own private 15" gauge line set off with the engine at a brisk pace. One of the Whorlton staff ran after the engine shouting in no uncertain terms that he was going too fast! It was used on the typical WLR formation of three yellow open bogie coaches. Ridley, Raymond's son, remembers it as a strong, powerful locomotive.

After leaving Whorlton it went to Ravenglass, Romney, Bressingham then in 2010 to Station Road Steam, Metheringham, Lincs. Sadly, it seems not to have worked since the early 1980s. The current owners started to restore it then a notice on their website indicated they had enough projects and were open to offers. Hopefully, one day someone will return this fine engine to steam.

In the 1980s a Barnes 'Atlantic' and a Severn Lamb 'Rio Grande' diesel worked at Whorlton but no more visiting engines came. Neither did any after the site was sold in 1990 and diesel WENDY was the only motive power.

SMOKEY JOE, the first steam engine on the revived Thorpe Light Railway, at the unloading area by the far loop, June 2013.
Anthony Coulls

Though the Lido closed for good in 2005 and the railway slumbered a revival of the line got under way in 2012. During the second volunteer working day in April BESSIE was delivered on loan. This was essentially a small dumper truck adapted to a rail chassis. It became a valuable works loco and the passenger locomotive until joined by a 'Rio Grande' diesel in 2016. For the opening planned in June 2013 Anthony Coulls who had spearheaded the revival planned something more appropriate - and more impressive - a visiting steam locomotive.

No. 1 SMOKEY JOE came from the Sherwood Forest Railway (SFR) the day before (re)opening day of what is now titled the Thorpe Light Railway. This Bagnall-style 0-4-0ST+T was built by K. Hardy in 1991 and ran on a private line in his garden in Cheltenham along with PET which he also built. The former had also run on the Cleethorpes Coast Light Railway. Mr Hardy's line was said to be a tight 'S' formation. When they were advertised for sale in 1998 David Colley bought them. As the SFR website says they were run up and down outside his garage now and then. When the Colley family built and opened the SFR in 2000 they started working there.

It arrived at Thorpe on Saturday June 22nd and was given a proving run round the circuit by the Colley's younger son Bob. Next day, 23rd, for the grand reopening elder brother David drove the first public train. SMOKEY JOE with two of the loaned Severn Lamb carriages alternated departures with BESSIE and the third carriage. With all carriages decked with bunting SMOKEY JOE carried a "Thorpe Pioneer" headboard while the diesel carried "Thorpe Explorer". With trains constant from 10 am so popular was the reopening that they ran past 4 pm until 4.30. Then the steam visitor was taken to the far (eastern) loop for loading and was soon back on its way home. It's two day visit marks it as the shortest stay of any visiting locomotive.

Various boiler problems like a weeping foundation ring mean that SMOKEY JOE has not been used for three years. The boiler is 25 years old and it is more cost effective to build a new one. The engine rests in the SFR workshops while a new boiler is on order.

Reopening day! The bunting is out as No. 1 SMOKEY JOE with the "Thorpe Pioneer" by-passes the station as resident BESSIE and open coach await the next departure for the "Thorpe Explorer."

Anthony Coulls

Test running the day before reopening as SMOKEY JOE and the three Severn Lamb carriages which had arrived a day earlier go round the near loop.

Anthony Coulls

SOONY by the unloading area in the far loop, August 24th 2014.

Anthony Coulls

In 2014 No. 27 SOONY arrived. This rather diminutive Baldwin-style 0-4-0 carried a 1901 worksplate but was actually completed in 2012. Courtesy of the Joe Nemeth Engineering website and a Miniature Railway Forum we find that it was a Baldwin design of 1903 with Hillcrest Shops, Reedley, California designing the miniature version. The engine's owner, Jamie Page, bought the drawings and castings from Hillcrest and started to build it himself at home in Wiltshire. After a time he outsourced it to professionals because his work as an airline pilot limited his time and it was a step up from his model engineering. The boiler was built by Glo'ster, the tender tank by Bromyard Services of Newport, Shropshire and the wheelsets by Alan Keef of Ross-on-Wye. It was delivered to Joe Nemeth near Bristol as a rolling chassis with cylinders partly assembled. Joe and son Dan completed it. A steel cab rather than a wooden one was built. The wheel profile is the same as Ravenglass' so it can run almost anywhere. It usually resides at the Perrygrove Railway in Gloucestershire whose then owner called it "a powerful little engine" having tackled with one carriage its 1,200 yard circuit with 1 in 30 banks. It visited the Fairbourne and Evesham Vale lines for their galas.

It was delivered to Thorpe on August 20th 2014 and taken by BESSIE to the shed. Three days later it was steamed up then taken round the circuit with one carriage then a second was added as it did another seven trips. The engine was very responsive to the regulator and the steady chuff from its chimney was a delight to hear. The open day on Sunday 24th had SOONY doing 27 passenger trains with its two carriages, this being nearly 12 miles. It proved very popular. Several days later the Kirklees LR crew who brought it then took it back to Perrygrove via a weekend's running at Kirklees' own gala.

For 2015 it was a change from miniature

(*Above*) SOONY steaming up outside the shed on August 23rd 2014 for test runs before the open day. It is seen (*below*) with one of the Severn Lamb carriages on one of the test runs crossing the bridge near the end of the far loop.

Both: Anthony Coulls

EFFIE and the two roofed Severn Lamb carriages towards the end of the near loop and heading for the station, July 26th 2015.
Philip Champion

outline to 'minimum gauge' as Heywood replica EFFIE arrived on June 24th. While the original was built in 1875 this replica was built by Great Northern Steam of Darlington in 1999 for David Humphrey. It has visited Ravenglass and Rhyl for galas but usually resides at the Cleethorpes Coast Light Railway. Here it typically hauls four Severn Lamb carriages but has managed nine. Just as the original acquired a tender after a few years so did the replica when its second owner built one in his garage.

On the 27th its driver from Cleethorpes, Aaron, steamed it up. BESSIE pulled it round the circuit seven times to help raise steam. Aaron drove it round another seven times hauling two carriages then adding a third one which had just been repaired for another three runs. Next he did steam driver training for some Thorpe volunteers. On Sunday 28th BESSIE did the early runs as EFFIE raised steam. Then all afternoon it worked 24 passenger trains followed by another half dozen, mainly for steam driver training. Many local people knew we were running steam as they had heard the shrill whistle echo across the river valley the previous afternoon. Seeing the driver stand up in the footplate well rather than sitting down was novel for our passengers. As with all steam engines EFFIE was popular with both the public and Thorpe volunteers. When driving it the odd sensation was for the upper part of the body to be cool in the summer breeze while the legs were really hot from the firebox. For July 26th's open day a volunteer brought along a generator to raise steam more quickly. A preserved Land Rover fire tender owned by another member and parked at the station obviated the need to go off to the shed for refilling with a hose. This time all 32 passenger trains were hauled by EFFIE. During its stay it ran about 85 circuits which is over 37 miles..

Resident locomotives for 2016 were

EFFIE and train leaving the far loop and heading up along the 'straight section' on a day of test running, June 27th 2015.

Anthony Coulls

Unloading EFFIE at the far loop, June 24th 2015.

Philip Champion

SOONY and train passing the lake in the far loop during its 2016 visit on September 4th that year.

Philip Champion

a Severn Lamb 'Rio 'Grande' diesel and BESSIE. Steam returned with SOONY. A few days after arrival in July it did a few test runs. A bolt from the motion shot out on Sunday 17th while going off shed so the Rio Grande' pulled trains for the first 90 minutes while a replacement was sourced. When SOONY did appear for a test circuit with all three carriages the platform was full of people eagerly watching it come with many taking photos. Its first trains were particularly busy. Another open day on August 21st had steam on all trains. An extra running day for the Friends on September 4th was covered by SOONY too. Altogether it did some 70 circuits during its 2016 stay.

Driving training under supervision was undertaken after public trains had ended. While the engine looks small it has plenty of power. This was particularly seen when coming out of a dip in the far loop then climbing whilst completing the curve and a straight section but slowing to 5 mph for a new bridge and the far loop points. SOONY managed the gradients capably and was soon able to recover from it. In fact, its steady chuff round the circuit sounded particularly satisfying. The engine won many admirers during its stay.

After two months it returned to Perrygrove. Currently work is being done on its motion.

Visiting steam engines provide extra interest today just as they did on the old Whorlton Lido Railway days - both for railway staff and the public. Negotiations are advanced for this year's visitors which should give even more interest for our third Sunday of the month running days. Details when confirmed will be posted on the Thorpe Light Railway website.

RESTORING A COMPRESSED AIR LOCO
by Rob Needham

The restored Eimco 401 in action with a loaded tipper wagon during the Lea Bailey Open Day on 17th September 2016.
All photos by the Author

Following restoration of the Eimco 12B rockershovel to working order (see *Summer Special 3*) during 2015 and the loan of 0-4-0CA ISSING SID from Statfold to Lea Bailey for the open weekend in May 2015, the small group involved at Lea Bailey decided that we would like a compressed air loco of our own. In January 2016 Patrick Keef pointed out to me an advert on the www.ingr.co.uk website for an ex-US compressed air loco for sale for £5750 ono. Apparently the seller had been trying to sell it for 18-24 months, so would probably accept a lower offer. But by the time I got home and checked the website – it had been sold!

A few days later, having a chat with Bryan Lawson at Alan Keef Ltd, he had found out that there is an Eimco loco in the UK, owned by Nick Kelly. Coincidentally I received an email from Nick Kelly about his Eimco 401 loco, inviting me to visit Isfield to see his loco, plus the Tramaire loco (the one from the www.ingr.co.uk advert) to see it before it left for Graz (Austria). Impressed by our restoration of the 12B, before I visited Isfield Nick offered the Eimco to us at Lea Bailey on a 2 year loan.

So on 24th April three of us from Lea Bailey travelled down to Isfield in a hired van to collect the loco. We were too late to see the Tramaire, which had left a couple of days earlier. When ISSING SID had been returned to Statfold the previous year, unloading had been easy, using two lifting strops slung from the forks of a forklift. There was a forklift at Isfield, with operator, so we planned to use the same method to load the

The loco as delivered from Canada on pallet. Taken at Isfield before transfer to Lea Bailey.

loco at Isfield. But the forklift turned out to be only half the height of that at Statfold, so it did not have the clearance below the forks to lift the Eimco. We admired the Eimco, confirmed that it was 18 inch gauge, and returned to Lea Bailey empty handed.

Plan B was to use a trailer. One of our members, Gareth from Salisbury, had a LWB LandRover and two-axle trailer. He offered to collect the Eimco and take it to Lea Bailey for our open day on 15th May. Meanwhile I had been to our local hydraulic supplier, Suttons of Ross, to see about getting some necessary parts, such as a UK air coupling and a pressure gauge, to replace the US coupling and u/s pressure gauge.

Late on the 15th, Gareth drew up at Lea Bailey to be welcomed by several interested members. Fortunately, as it turned out, he had decided not to try to re-gauge the loco before loading it on the trailer. Unloading at Lea Bailey was relatively easy. At the end of the day we left if resting on some old sleepers.

The following Sunday (our working days at Lea Bailey usually being Sundays) we started work. The air coupling and pressure gauge were replaced with new. A quick check showed that some work would be needed on the hand-brake. Assuming that the air-motor (a Type 200, the same model as on the 12B rockershovel) and gearbox were in working order, the main task would be to re-gauge to 2ft. Work started by removing the drive chains and the chain guard. Our only guide was a copy of the Eimco operator's manual, found and downloaded from the internet. The main help this gave was a series of illustrations with a list of parts. But, no problem, we had been told that the advice from the Canadian contractor from whom the loco had been bought was that it was only a couple of hours work to re-gauge. Many times over the following six months was this advice ironically commented upon. The loco had reportedly last worked in Canada in 2012, and when delivered to Isfield there was still some air in the tank. So we hoped that getting the loco working at Lea Bailey would be straightforward.

The work to get the loco working can be

summarized as (but not necessarily in this order):
1. Remove handbrake and refit to suit 2ft gauge
2. Remove chains and guard to enable access to axles
3. Remove axleboxes and axles
4. Remove wheels from axles, re-arrange spacers on axles so that gauge set to 2ft
5. Press wheels on to axles
6. Fit new bearings and seals on axles
7. Refit axleboxes
8. Refit re-gauged wheels/axleboxes/axles to loco
9. Refit drive chains and guard
10. Replace air hoses between control valve and motor
11. Repair drivers seat
12. Fit (new) whistle
13. Get air tank pressure tested and certified by qualified engineer
14. When loco is on 2ft gauge track, tow it along in gear to check air motor rotates freely
15. Check operation of gearbox and check oil levels (motor and gearbox)
16. Ready for first powered run

Above: The unrestored footplate, note the air coupling and pressure gauge.

Below: The new air coupling, pressure gauge and whistle.

PARTS LIST FOR EIMCO 401 AIR LOCOMOTIVE   The Eimco Corporation, Salt Lake City 10, Utah, U.S.A.

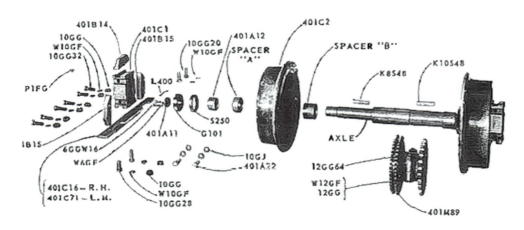

REAR AXLE GROUP

(FOR GAUGE & GROUP NO. SEE CHART BELOW)

Part No.	Quan.	Description
401C1	2	Rear Journal Box
401C2	2	Wheel
401A11	2	Keeper Plate
401A12	2	Bearing Spacer
401B14	2	Guide
401B15	4	Bracket
401C16	1	Retainer – Right Side
See List	1	Axle
401A22	8	Adjusting Bolt
401C71	1	Retainer – Left Side
401M89	1	Sprocket Assembly
		Includes:
12GG64	2	Cap Screw
W12GF	2	Lock Washer
12GG	2	Nut

Part No.	Quan.	Description
See List	—	Gauge Spacers "A" & "B"
G101	2	Bearing
K8S48	2	Key
K10540	1	Key
L400	1	Lock Wire
P1FG	2	Grease Fitting
S250	2	Seal
6GGW16	4	Cap Screw
W6GF	4	Lock Washer
10GG20	2	Cap Screw
10GG28	6	Cap Screw
10GG32	12	Cap Screw
W10GF	20	Lock Washer
10GG	18	Nut
10GJ	16	Jam Nut

REAR AXLE GAUGE, SPACER & AXLE LIST

Complete Axle Group	Gauge		Spacer "A"		Spacer "B"		Axle
	inches	m.m.	Part Number	Quan.	Part Number	Quan.	Part Number
401M24	18	460	401A3	2	—	0	401C19
401M182	18-3/8	467	401A180	2	401A179	2	401C19
401M159	19-5/8	500	401A160	2	401A161	2	401C19
401M116	20	510	401A114	2	401A115	2	401C19
401M116	22	560	401A115	2	401A114	2	401C19
401M159	22-3/8	570	401A161	2	401A160	2	401C19
401M182	23-5/8	600	401A179	2	401A180	2	401C19
401M24	24	610	—	0	401A3	2	401C19
401M227	30	760	—	0	401A3	2	401C229

BE SURE TO GIVE SERIAL NUMBER OF LOCOMOTIVE WHEN ORDERING PARTS

Eimco 401 locomotive parts list & instruction book page 18.

Above: The air hoses between motor and control valve.

Below: Fitting the drain cock to clear air from top of water-filled air tank.

Unfortunately, some items on the list took rather longer than expected. Most nuts and bolts were sufficiently corroded as to need replacement. Fortunately (and to our surprise) all turned out to be metric. The Eimco manual illustrations were useful for identifying parts, but not much more. Knowing that we needed a spring with Eimco part number 15A1355 was not much use as we could find no one supplying parts for Eimco 401 locos. Much more useful was having Alan Keef's works just down the road where Bryan Lawson could often find something equivalent to the parts we wanted in their stores.

After two days working on the loco, we had both axles removed ready for re-gauging. Two weeks later they had been re-gauged by Alan Keef (after our attempts to remove the wheels from the axles with a sledgehammer had failed miserably – 3 hours to move one wheel ¼ inch) using their mobile wheel press – an impressive machine rescued many years ago from the old Motor Rail works. But it then took another 6 weeks work to get the first re-gauged axle back on the loco. And another two weeks to get the second axle in place. Then we found that clearance between each wheel and the loco frame was almost non-existent - to get one wheel to rotate we had to grind some metal off the wheel. The machining of the axleboxes was also found to be rather rough, requiring some fettling before one axlebox would accept the bearing and seal.

When finished, the final task was to get the air tank pressure tested before we could give the loco a powered test run. Graham Morris agreed to do the testing, but first we had to get the loco ready. We needed a drain cock modifying (with a 3ft pipe) and fitting to the air tank so that when full of water all air could be removed from the top of the tank, there being no opening in the tank above the mid point where a drain cock could be fitted. With drain cock fitted we filled the tank with water (having removed the control valve and fitted a temporary blind flange in its place), and pumped it up to 165psi (= operating pressure + 50%). After leaving it to settle and checking that all air had been removed, there was no sign of any leaks. So we left the loco locked away for 7 days. When checked a week later, the pressure gauge was still indicating 150psi. So the following day Graham came and, after we had drained the water from the tank, conducted the pressure test to 110psi. Success! So we had the required certificate. Time for a few last minute tasks, such as refitting the manhole cover on the air tank (the bolt had failed when opening the cover for Graham to inspect the interior of the tank aft the pressure test. Finally we were ready for the loco to perform at our open day on 17th September for its owner, Nick Kelly. After brief thought we named it WHISTLING PIG, because apparently low-pressure air locos are known in the US as whistle pigs, and the Forest of Dean has a sizeable population of wild boar (we have seen them at Lea Bailey), so it seemed an apt name.

Come and see the loco running at Lea Bailey this year! There will be a Compressed Air Gala on 13th / 14th May, when ISSING SID will be visiting from Statfold, and our fifth anniversary event is provisionally planned for 16th September.

REGAUGING THE WHEELS

Above Left: The ex-Simplex wheel press at Alan Keef works.

Above: The wheels being set to 2ft gauge on the wheel press.

Left: The regauged wheels, with new bearings in place.

Below: Lowering the regauged loco on to the track at Lea Bailey.

Above: The restored loco posed with 'miners' in the entrance to Lea Bailey gold mine.

Below: Owner Nick Kelly drives his loco at Lea Bailey during the Open Day on 17th September.

TIME FOR A HALT
Photographs by Peter Donovan

It has become quite fashionable in recent years for the Welsh narrow gauge lines to enhance the appearance of some of their wayside stopping places. These examples are (*above*) at Heniarth on the Welshpool & Llanfair and Nantyronen (*left*) on the Vale of Rheidol.